SOR JUANA

Latinx Pop Culture

SERIES EDITORS

Frederick Luis Aldama and Arturo J. Aldama

SOR JUANA

Or, The Persistence of Pop

Ilan Stavans

THE UNIVERSITY OF
ARIZONA PRESS

TUCSON

The University of Arizona Press
www.uapress.arizona.edu

ISBN-13: 978-0-8165-3607-8 (paper)

Cover design by Leigh McDonald
Cover art: Lena Bartula, *Los secretos* (2010)

Library of Congress Cataloging-in-Publication Data
Names: Stavans, Ilan, author.
Title: Sor Juana : or, the persistence of pop / Ilan Stavans.
Other titles: Latinx pop culture.
Description: Tucson : The University of Arizona Press, 2018. | Series: Latinx pop
    culture
Identifiers: LCCN 2017060971 | ISBN 9780816536078 (pbk. : alk. paper)
Subjects: LCSH: Juana Inés de la Cruz, Sister, 1651–1695. | Juana Inés de la Cruz,
    Sister, 1651–1695—Criticism and interpretation. | Nuns—Mexico—Biography. |
    LCGFT: Biographies.
Classification: LCC PQ7296.J6 Z8928 2018 | DDC 861/.3 [B] —dc23 LC record
    available at https://lccn.loc.gov/2017060971

Printed in the United States of America
♾ This paper meets the requirements of ANSI/NISO Z39.48-1992 (Permanence of
Paper).

To Angelina Muníz-Huberman

"One cannot undo fame."

—ANONYMOUS

CONTENTS

SOR JUANA

I entered
the convent
because I
understood
the state
of affairs

(I speak of the accessory, not the formal ones),

many repugnant

to my temper

and because,

with the total

negation

I had

for marriage,

it was

the least

disproportionate,

in

terms

of security

for my salvation,

to
which
the
impertinence

of my demeanor

ceded my full

respect,

which was   to want

to live

alone

1
THE FINAL SCREAM

She shows up as a *guerrillera*, with rifle and bullet belts. Or replaces the screamer in Edvard Munch's famous expressionist painting of 1910. She dances in heaven with Marc Chagall's ethereal characters. Stands next to the Beatles and other added luminaries in *Sgt. Pepper's Lonely Hearts Club Band*. Wears a shoulder tattoo. Is the protagonist of a telenovela. Or a 1993 opera. The target of countless homages by literati such as Gabriela Mistral, Amado Nervo, Xavier Villaurrutia, and José Lezama Lima. A play mounted by the Royal Shakespeare Company, staged in Stratford-upon-Avon in 2012. A Halloween custom. And an animated TV series.

Even more frequently, she is paid tribute to in *ranchera*, *tejano*, and hip-hop lyrics. Is on a stamp. And, between 1988 and 1992, on the $1,000 peso bill, which was pushed out by inflation, becoming the $200 peso note, also with her semblance. She is a doll. A piñata. Drops by in high heels. Is on T-shirts. On expensive watches. Chillin' next to an open book. And, frequently, chatting on her iPhone.

The conduits keep multiplying: statues, Lotería cards, key chains, recipe books, coffee mugs, Día de los Muertos costumes . . . Along with Ernesto "Che" Guevara and Evita Perón, she is ubiquitous.

Ironically, Juana de Asbaje—alias Sor Juana de la Cruz—died in anonymity. Her grave was unmarked for almost three hundred years, until the 1970s, when the Convent of Santa Paula of the Order of San Jerónimo, where she spent her last years, underwent renovation and her remains were purportedly identified. It was a symbolic moment, since she was firmly grounded in the pantheon of Mexican icons. A few years later, Octavio Paz would publish a landmark—if controversial—biography, *Sor Juana: Or, The Traps of Faith* (1982), portraying her as a key intellectual figure in the journey of Latin America toward modernity, which in his view "is still an unhealed wound."

Even with the honorific "the Tenth Muse," it would surely surprise her to come across the iconographic machine she has nurtured. In the land of "bad hombres," she is a rabble-rouser. A vocal one. Virginia Woolf once said: "The truth is, I often like women. I like their unconventionality. I like their completeness. I like their anonymity." The truth is, after her death nothing related to Sor Juana is anonymous.

"What . . . is the devil in my being a woman?" And "How was I to endure? An uncommon sort of martyrdom in which I was both martyr and executioner." She made these statements in her famous epistolary memoir, *Response to the Most Illustrious Poetess Sor Filotea de la Cruz*. (Unless otherwise noted, these and other English translations are by Margaret Sayers Peden, from Sor Juana Inés de la Cruz's *Poems, Protest, and a Dream* [1998].) She also wondered: Am I, by virtue of my gender, condemned to eternal silence, as "is intended not only for women, but for *all* incompetents"? Isn't silence a form of compliance, the art of saying without saying?

These queries form the vertebrae of her literary contribution and sit perfectly well in a courageous document that serves both as a mirror to her overall odyssey and as a farewell letter. In poor health and besieged by the merciless campaign of intimidation her superiors were orchestrating, she drafted her uneasy lines meticulously, as if aware that she was signing her own death sentence. She was forty-three.

Until a few months earlier, her star had shone bright and high. Time and again she had challenged the male-dominated intellectual milieu, emerging triumphant to the applause of one viceregal court after another. While she was occasionally confronted by a prioress, cautioned by her confessor against sacrilegious misconduct, and reprimanded by a representative of the archbishop of Mexico, Francisco Aguiar y Seijas, her position in the Convent of Santa Paula was secure. And her reputation as the premier Baroque poet in New Spain, as Mexico was known in the seventeenth century, reached far beyond—from Quito to Lima, from the Philippines to the Iberian Peninsula.

But now, sequestered in her convent cell, she was alone and lonely. As she drafted her response, dated March 1, 1691, she knew her fate was no longer in her hands. The delicate balance that she had successfully maintained most of her adult life had finally collapsed. Envy and resentment surrounded her. So she made sure her double message was unclouded. She confessed her "insignificance" as a woman, her "vile nature," her "unworthiness." She did so mainly because she wished "no quarrel with the Holy Office, for I am ignorant, and I tremble that I may express some proposition that will cause offense or twist the true meaning of some scripture." However, she seized the occasion to denounce openly the repressive, misogynistic atmosphere that surrounded her and the criticism that had targeted her as a poet.

Sor Juana first used her response to articulate a persuasive manifesto in favor of intellectual rights for women, a topic that had preoccupied her since childhood; and then, so as not to alienate her superiors, she promised to entrust her future to her addressee: "You will command what I am to do," she told Sor Filotea de la Cruz, aware, no doubt, that complete silence and a full abstention from all literary endeavors would be requested of her. And she would comply. "I will weaken and dull the workings of my feeble reason," she wrote; that is, not a single *redondilla*, not a single epigraph more would come out of her pen.

Never again would she participate in poetry contests, never would she accept commissions to celebrate a government official. Eventually this silence also meant selling her much-admired collection of indigenous and imported musical instruments and dismantling her considerable library, which contemporary scholars, including Pedro Henríquez Ureña, Dorothy Schons, Ermilo Abreu Gómez, Tarsicio Herrera Zapién, and Francisco de la Maza, have estimated to comprise four hundred to four thousand volumes, no small number for a time when book publishing was still a most elitist affair and the circulation of works of literature, religion, and philosophy was restricted in the Spanish colonies.

Judging by the standards of conformity and resignation, Sor Juana's letter is incredibly candid. She is neither sorry nor remorseful. She drafts it as a *j'accuse*, a map to the many obstacles she has found on the road to knowledge and self-assertion. And time has added relevance to her double message, turning the document into a cornerstone of Hispanic American identity: it is at once a chronicle of the tense gender relations in the Western hemisphere, a rich portrait of the social behavior that prevailed more than a century before independence from Spain was gained in 1810, and the very first intellectual autobiography written by a criolla in an ecosystem known for its solipsism, introversion, and allergy to public confessions.

While she wrote it as a private letter, she had reason to believe it would become a civic affront, and so she let herself go. Sick, anxious, persecuted by visible ghosts, Sor Juana allowed herself *un último grito*—a final scream, a shriek of desperation—promising afterward to lose herself forever in the passive piety forced by the Catholic Church on scores of anonymous nuns.

2

THE GREATEST FINEZA

Modernity is about shared recognition. In the pantheon of modern Mexican icons, which includes the versatile *calavera* popularized by José Guadalupe Posada, conquistador Hernán Cortés's La Malinche, mestizo president Benito Juárez, revolutionary hero Emiliano Zapata, downtrodden movie star Cantinflas, pachuco rebel Tin Tan, the artistic couple Diego Rivera and Frida Kahlo, and neo-Zapatista radical Subcomandante Marcos, Sor Juana holds a unique place. This, to a large extent, is the result of her ecclesiastical connections.

One example: At Stanford University's Stern Dining Hall, in a famous painting by José Antonio Burciaga called *Last Supper of Chicano Heroes*—a tribute to Leonardo da Vinci's fifteenth-century *L'ultima cena*—on the Casa Zapata side, where Burciaga and his wife were resident fellows between 1985 and 1994, Sor Juana is in the front row, along with Zapata, Juárez, Cesar Chavez, and other luminaries. At the bottom of the mural, on the tablecloth, it reads: ". . . and to all those who died, scrubbed floors, wept, and fought for us." The number of women is minuscule. Dolores Huerta, for one, is not far. But above everyone and right in the center is the Virgin of Guadalupe.

In her religious attire, Sor Juana is stolid, emotionless, and, yes, cool. "As long as she thinks as a man," Virginia Woolf announced, "no one objects to a woman thinking." But though Sor Juana is silent, in the image she clearly doesn't think as a man. She thinks as herself, that is, as a woman.

Modernity is also about endless reproducibility. It is about refashioning a product while testing its limits. And it is about consumerism. Buying is a form of appropriation. Packaging Sor Juana into merchandise is part of Mexico's modernization project. In a nation obsessed with masks depicting its own divided self—part indigenous, part European—and a progeny shaped in testosterone, she is the unsilenced sister. She is also a motif of contained eroticism. In the popular imagination, the portrayals of her oscillate between absolute chastity and explosive lasciviousness.

In other words, she is visceral and intuitive as well as shrewd and even ingenious. In the context of the deep-rooted devotion to another omnipresent image in Mexico, the Virgin of Guadalupe, Sor Juana symbolizes the need for theological flexibility.

Indeed, Mexico, known as the land of innuendos, needs a repressed dissident like her, beautiful in her tenacity and tenacious in her beauty. A heroine apparently disdainful of her own mission: to expose male brutality, not through out-and-out violence, but by means of discreet, carefully calibrated argument.

Although the roots of Sor Juana's serious quarrels with the church establishment can be traced back more than a decade earlier, her discontent reached an apex in 1690, as she sat down to write an argument against a celebrated Portuguese Jesuit, Father Antonio de Vieyra, one of the most eloquent and distinguished Christian thinkers and orators of the seventeenth century, admired especially in Spain and Mexico.

On Holy Thursday of 1650, at the Royal Chapel in Lisbon, Vieyra had delivered an erudite sermon on one of Jesus Christ's important *finezas*, a term used to describe divine acts of loving-kindness toward humankind. Such speculative topics were often at the center of heated theological debates in Spain and Portugal, and, as in Father Vieyra's case, these debates produced decades-long repercussions in their American colonies.

Even a quick glance at the sermon makes Father Vieyra's narrative and rhetorical talents clear: he is lucid yet verbose, insightful yet manipulative in regard to the information he is handling. He quotes generously from Saint John Chrysostom, Saint Thomas Aquinas, and Saint Augustine, but he takes issue with each and every one of these thinkers, claiming they failed to understand the meaning behind Christ's decisive *fineza*: his washing the feet of his disciples, including those of Judas, toward the end of his days.

On the other side of the Atlantic, almost four decades later, Sor Juana discussed Father Vieyra's thesis during an academic gathering in a cloister of her Convent of Santa Paula of the Order of San Jerónimo, located in the southern section of today's Mexico City, then a placid urban center with a population of some one hundred thousand. She praised Father Vieyra's wisdom and applauded his scope but sharply criticized his understanding of Christ's love for humanity. She accused him of misunderstanding Christ's most important *fineza*: according to Father Vieyra, Christ had washed his disciples' feet for love's own sake; Sor Juana, on the other hand, viewed the act as evidence of Christ's love for humanity.

This distinction might seem insignificant, especially to contemporary readers, but in seventeenth-century Mexico it was extremely controversial. Sor Juana embellished her quasi-heretical argument with Greek and Latinate quotes and biblical references; she placed it in the context of other crucial arguments, such as the distinction between love and utility and the theme of "negative favors." In her characteristic Baroque style, in which appearances are deceitful and light and shadow are versions of each other, she claims: "We appreciate and we ponder the exquisiteness of divine love, in which to reward is a benefaction and to chastise is a benefaction, and the absence of benefaction is the greatest benefaction, and the absence of a *fineza* is the greatest *fineza*."

Don Manuel Fernández de Santa Cruz y Sahagún, the bishop of Puebla, a clergyman close to Sor Juana and a rival of Francisco Aguiar y Seijas, archbishop of Mexico since 1681 and known for his relentless misogyny, asked her to write down her thoughts. The result was the *Athenagoric Letter*, as elegant, punctilious, and exhausting an address as she was capable of and among her most lucid pieces of writing, a treatise not only on theology but on ecclesiastical politics as well. It circulated unofficially for a short while until the bishop of Puebla, without Sor Juana's permission, had the treatise titled and privately printed, at his own expense, in late November 1690.

He even sent a copy to Sor Juana herself, with a personal dedication. Because of her celebrity, news of her critique of Father Vieyra was soon widespread. Her supporters applauded her audacity and determination, but her opponents accused her of insolence and disrespect to a luminary whose authority could not be denied. Her straightforward commentary generated an atmosphere of fear. Rumors and insinuations abounded, while the specter of the Holy Office loomed in the background. Her superiors were not impressed: they judged her female imprudence regrettable and looked for ways to punish her.

Soon the bishop of Puebla himself, either by his own personal choice or encouraged by higher authorities, decided to write a letter to Sor Juana. The epistle is short, strong, and uncompromising. He asks her to give up her secularism, to devote herself to faith, and to abandon the careless roads of reason. His comments, surprisingly, are more threatening than they might appear at first sight. Maintaining a correspondence, as Sor Juana did with innumerable people in Mexico and beyond, was not the private affair we have grown accustomed to. Letters easily reached more eyes than those of the parties involved, so the correspondent was usually compelled to manipulate language and meaning, to insinuate and allude, to hide behind formulaic jargon—in short, to apply a self-censoring device so as not to become the subject of public embarrassment. Fernández de Santa Cruz addresses Sor Juana as *señora mía* (my lady) and *Vuestra merced* (Your Reverence). He grants her respect and distinction, and he shows a high degree of admiration for and familiarity with her work, but he also wants her rebellious spirit brought under control and alludes to the fragility of her situation as a woman in a male-controlled environment. In spite of the fact that her *Athenagoric Letter* is a religious disquisition, the bishop of Puebla asks her to put aside her nearsighted scientific pursuits in favor of what nuns ought to do: devote themselves to the purest of spiritual practices—their marital love for Jesus Christ.

"I don't pretend, in this epistle, for Y. R. to change your talents by renouncing books, but to improve them by occasionally reading that of Jesus Christ," writes Fernández de Santa Cruz, so that Sor Juana's nature, "well-endowed by the Almighty with many positive aspects on this earth, will not have to grant her a negative condemnation in the world to come." The last paragraph is a display of sexual innuendo:

"These [improvements] I wish to Y. R., for since I kissed your hand many years ago, I live in love with your soul, and this love has not been cooled by time or distance, because spiritual love is not overcome by transitoriness, and is recognizable only when it is focused toward growth. Let my supplications be heard by Y. R. May they mark you a saint and keep you for all posterity."

On the surface Fernández de Santa Cruz's letter seems cordial: he is at once tolerant and reprimanding, lenient and severe; on a deeper level, however, the text is a more sophisticated stratagem—an authoritarian masquerade, an attack on Sor Juana's overall character, an accusation vibrating with sexual transgression. To be more comfortable, to express himself without inhibition, the bishop of Puebla chose to write under a pseudonym: Sor Filotea de la Cruz. Oscar Wilde argued once that man is least himself when he talks in his own person. Give him a mask, and he will tell you the truth. The irony couldn't be more obvious: Fernández de Santa Cruz attacks Sor Juana at her most vulnerable point, her womanhood, but from a woman's perspective; that is, he suggests she has trespassed into the male order and he in turn must stop her by entering the female realm.

One can say, of course, that Fernández de Santa Cruz, sympathetic as he is to Sor Juana, is tempering the severity of his message by pretending to be a sister nun instead of a male superior. But this argument misses the irony behind the masquerade: the accuser assumes the voice of the accused in order to punish her; he impersonates a woman to stop her own move toward the male world. Sor Juana surely knew the true identity of her interlocutor; nevertheless, she chose to play the game. "My most illustrious *señora. . . ,*" she begins her *Response to Sor Filotea.* "And thus say I, most honorable lady. Why do I receive such favor?" Since Fernández de Santa Cruz had already transgressed her right to privacy by printing the *Athenagoric Letter,* she would respond by exhibiting her guilt in public, by detailing her torturous journey, by openly discussing her lifelong impersonations.

This elaborate prank is at the center of Sor Juana's career. The environment had forced a thespian defense mechanism upon her. She had become an impersonator of masculinity, an actress pretending to be someone other than herself. To allow her intellectual talents to flourish, she had to revamp, even reinvent, her feminine side. This, of course, has generated a flurry of modern psychological studies. The most controversial is by a German scholar, Ludwig Pfandl, whose book, *Juana Inés de la Cruz, die zehnte Muse von Mexico* (1946), drew on the theories of Sigmund Freud to offer a range of reductive explanations of Sor Juana's conduct. Pfandl described her as a "neurotic with an Oedipal complex," a frustrated woman, vengeful, jealous, and malign. Others have ventured similar, if not quite so extreme, interpretations, portraying the nun as hysterical and sexually repressed.

These simplistic views reflected the times in which they were concocted. Certainly, Sor Juana's lifelong struggle for individual expression evidenced admirable equanimity. Given the limited space she had in which to act, she was both ingenious and astute about finding alternative strategies of fulfillment. In fact, one might argue she was at times too tame, too cautious, too conscious of her limits and limitations, too conservative in her approach to truly defy the ecclesiastical status quo.

Her confrontation with the church is not unlike that which artists and intellectuals experience when denouncing the nearsightedness of the society in which they live. While in her *Response to Sor Filotea* she articulated a clear defense of secularism, she was also careful not to become a dissident, an apostate, a Joan of Arc facing an inevitable death by burning. The epistle might have been an occasion for self-reflection, but it wasn't a threat to secede. Sor Juana was too subtle, too docile, and too submissive at heart; she was aware of the wide attention she attracted from various segments of society but was careful not to turn her performance into a public scandal.

Had she been more radical, less conciliatory, she could have provided a catalyst to reform and an invitation to secularism. But many factors impeded her. First and foremost is the fact that New Spain lacked a critical tradition. The Spanish-speaking Americas were not born in a struggle for liberalism and democracy. They inherited the Iberian philosophy of timidity and intolerance. Sor Juana challenged this philosophy, but ultimately she gave up her struggle.

Modern feminist criticism of Sor Juana disagrees. Georgina Sabat de Rivers, Marie-Cécile Bénassy-Berling, and Stephanie Merrim, three leading *sorjuanistas*, believe the tragic journey of the Mexican nun is attributable less to her own personal weakness than to the force of patriarchal structures. They appreciate Sor Juana's twisting literary course as weaving a "uniquely deviant, convoluted pathway between masculine and feminine modes."

The *Response to Sor Filotea*, they argue, is about balancing recognition and rejection. What matters is not the limits of her rebelliousness but the strategies she adopted in order to find what Virginia Woolf calls "a room of one's own" in her male-dominated society. Sor Juana should not be perceived as submissive, a flaccid promoter of enlightenment, since no clear reform could be attained in New Spain from *within* the ecclesiastical hierarchy.

Américo Castro, author of *The Structure of Spanish History* (1954), whose career in part focused on "Marranism," the experience of descendants of Jews whose families converted to Catholicism before, during, and after 1492, insinuates that Sor Juana might have been crypto-Jewish. In the words of Yirmiyahu Yovel, whose book *The Other Within: The Marranos, Split Identity and Emerging Modernity* (2009) studies the plight of this particular population in full, "Judaizers became increasingly lonely and secluded, depending more on the resources of their own solitary selves—on memory, hope, vision, and personal conviction. For them authentic religion had been deinstitutionalized and privatized—not merely in the sense that it was concealed inside the home, but also of depending on the inner heart as its almost sole support. . . . In the end, and all along, the person had to face the most important religious truths—decisions about value, and about personal fate in this and the next world—within a private 'inner forum.'" Sor Juana, if indeed she had Jewish blood, might have faced her personal demons within that "inner forum."

Among the countless visual tributes to Sor Juana, one of my favorite is Eko's sequence of engravings based on the *Response to Sor Filotea*. The legendary Mexican lithographer takes the portions about her rejecting marriage as an option, reimagining it as a sensual dialogue—perhaps with Sor Juana's benefactor, the Condesa de Paredes. A tacit suggestion, at once manifest and subdued, is made of her lesbianism.

The issue of Sor Juana's public scandal and the extent of her courage have gained clarity as a result of a major scholarly breakthrough. For a long time scholars believed the *Response to Sor Filotea* was her only overtly autobiographical work, but that view changed in 1981, when Father Aureliano Tapia Méndez published a booklet entitled *Sor Juana: A Spiritual Self-Defense*, in which he included a five-and-a-half-page letter he had uncovered in the Seminario Arquidiocesano of Monterrey, in northern Mexico. The letter, undated but probably written in 1681, was from Sor Juana to her confessor, Father Antonio Núñez de Miranda. At first its authenticity was questioned, but the style of the epistle and crucial information contained in it confirm its credibility and its relevance.

Far more candid than the *Response to Sor Filotea*, if less poetic, it shows that Sor Juana's confrontation with the church hierarchy predated the Vieyra controversy. In addition, it evidences the degree of intimacy she had with her confessor, who, as is clear in *A Spiritual Self-Defense*, had disparaged her in the circles of power; and it fully illustrates Sor Juana's changing steadfastness in that, probably as a result of the support she had earlier received from the viceregal court, she was far more confrontational, more self-assured and uncompromising, in 1681 than in 1690.

Sor Juana also addresses Father Núñez de Miranda as "Y[our] R[everence]." "For some time now," she writes, "various persons have informed me that I am singled out for censure in the conversations of Y. R., in which you denounce my actions with such bitter exaggeration as to suggest a *public scandal*." The basis for his complaint: her poetry, a most unworthy and profane endeavor in the eyes of the Catholic Church.

Her defense is clear-cut. "On which . . . occasions was the transgression of having written them so grave?" Sor Juana wonders. She then describes the pressure she experiences: "Women feel that men surpass them, and that I seem to place myself on a level with men; some wish that I did not know so much; others say that I ought to know more to merit such applause; elderly women do not wish that other women know more than they; young women, that others present a good appearance; and one and all wish me to conform to the rules of their judgment; so that from all sides comes such a singular martyrdom as I deem none other has ever experienced."

Her solution can be read as a diatribe against dogmatism in that it suggests an individualistic stand that, taken a step further, would bring laissez-faire reform. "I beg of Y. R.," Sor Juana writes, "that if you do not wish or find it in your heart to favor me (for that is voluntary) you think of me no more, for though I shall regret so great a loss, I shall utter no complaint, because God, Who created and redeemed me and Who has bestowed so many mercies on me, will supply a remedy in order that my soul, awaiting His kindness, shall not be lost even though it lack the direction of Y. R., for He has made many keys to Heaven and has not confined Himself to a single criterion; rather, there are many mansions of people of as many different natures, and in the world there are many theologians, but were they lacking, salvation lies more in the desiring than in the knowing, and that will be more in me than in my confessor."

Less than a decade later, though, her approach would be less defiant. While in both works Sor Juana claims to have built her literary career on the requests of others, in the *Response to Sor Filotea* she has become aware of her vulnerability. She writes a self-portrait designed to highlight her talents and scope. One of her mythological heroes, she notes, is Phaethon, son of Helios, the sun god, and the heroine Clymene, who wants only to drive his father's sun chariot for a day. Unable to control the horses that pull the chariot across the sky, he is killed and falls to earth when Zeus hurls a thunderbolt at him. The story of Phaethon's overreaching ambition is an allegory, of course, a mirror in which Sor Juana saw her own reflection. Her hunger for wisdom brought her glory, but it also—and she always knew it—would precipitate her downfall.

3

MEDALLION

Very few oil portraits of Sor Juana survive, all of them derivative and not fully reliable, in that they were painted after her death in 1695. Three stand out: those by the Mexican artists Juan de Miranda and Miguel Cabrera hang in the Universidad Nacional Autónoma de México and the fortress of Chapultepec, respectively; an anonymous third portrait now belongs to the Philadelphia Museum of Art. The impression given by the three is that of a proud elitist, a stoic, serious, visionary learner, a distinguished—and distinguishable—woman of substance.

Sor Juana is invariably at the center of the composition, immobile, wearing a habit resembling that of the Sisters of the Immaculate Conception: a white tunic with full but cuffed sleeves, a scapular, and a white coif and black veil completely concealing her hair. Below her chin is a huge metal or parchment medallion, nearly covering her neck, illustrated with a religious scene incorporating an angel. A black thong of the Order of San Agustín encircles her waist, and a rosary dangling from her neck almost reaches her knees. In Miranda's portrait she is standing and writing; in Cabrera's she sits, her right hand resting on a large book.

In contemporary art, the medallion plays a significant role. Rare is the Sor Juana likeness that excludes it. The oval artifact is a fertile ground for experimentation. At times it is a parenthetical space that features alternative messages the artist is interested in delivering. It also serves the role of mirror in which the nun sees herself reflected, occasionally in distorted ways. Of course, a medallion, in Sor Juana's time, was simultaneously used as an object of vanity and to portray a religious scene. This invites artists to use it as a springboard to reflect on female self-worth. It might also be seen as a black hole into which her quest at once vanishes and resurfaces in cyclical fashion.

As a result, the medallion, in and of itself, is arguably the item most closely associated with her, to the extent that sometimes shows up on its own, conjuring, like a Borgesian aleph, Sor Juana's entire universe. (A second item associated with her is the nun's habit.) In the 1970s, when her remains were apparently identified, the medallion was also supposedly found. Ipso facto, it was taken by Margarita López Portillo, sister of then-President José López Portillo, "for safekeeping," in her words. In 1995, as the tercentennial of Sor Juana's death was celebrated, a member of Congress asked that it be returned "to the Mexican people," a request with which Margarita López Portillo complied. However, no actual proof of authenticity, either at the time of the identification nor when it was returned, was ever established. In other words, the entire anecdote might be nothing but an urban legend.

In a popular Sor Juana doll made of yarn, the medallion is the largest feature. In an installation showing her on a bicycle, it almost looks like a knightly shade. And in a comic strip detailing her plight, the medallion is the repeating motif, a kind of talisman that travels with her as she faces adversity.

In any case, Sor Juana's religious attire and her crucifix are standard features in portraits of the time. Still, the fact that only her face is exposed is significant. Male religious icons in Mexican art, from Jesus Christ to the crowded panoply of saints and child angels, are often half-naked, as if male flesh needs to be displayed, represented, to convey the ethos of these figures. Think, foremost, of Jesus Christ: he is seldom in a tunic. Instead, he is unclothed, a symbol of purity, self-effacement, and unpretentiousness. But their female counterparts, from the Virgin of Guadalupe to La Malinche, almost without exception are totally dressed; their pure, original flesh is both threatening and threatened when exposed to the public eye. In the backdrop of each painting of Sor Juana, society and nature play absolutely no role. Neither animals nor people surround her—only books, ink, and pens.

In fact, modern scholars and biographers, such as Ermilo Abreu Gómez, have made inventories of Sor Juana's library based in part on the content of her work and on the portraits of her that survive. We know how well versed she was in El Siglo de Oro Español, the Golden Age of Spanish literature, particularly in the works of Luis de Góngora, whom she so admired. Also, the Baroque period in which she lived celebrated a handful of Hellenistic classics, most especially Ovid's *Metamorphoses*, and she was certainly well acquainted with Neoplatonic and Scholastic texts, most of which she probably read in anthologies, compendiums, encyclopedias, and dictionaries of deities and symbols of antiquity.

She was familiar with Avicenna, Aquinas, and Maimonides. Her poem "El sueño," as Octavio Paz shows in *The Traps of Faith*, manifests her considerable knowledge of Cicero and particularly of Athanasius Kircher's *Iter exstaticum coeleste*. She also read Macrobius, Baltasar de Vitoria, Juan Pérez de Moya, Boethius, and Boccaccio, as well as Pico della Mirandola, Pierio Valeriano's dictionary of symbols, the *Hieroglyphica*, and Tommaso Garzoni's *Piazza universale di tutte le professioni del mondo, e nobili e ignobili*, among others.

Books, Sor Juana claims in the *Response to Sor Filotea*, were her lifelong passion and her best, most loyal companions. In her eyes they were instruments of knowledge and control devised by humankind to make order from chaos. Her love for them was maternal: she embraced and collected them and gave birth to several poetry pamphlets circulated among friends and fans, as well as a set of three printed volumes, all published in Spain: *Castalian Inundation* (1689), *Works* (1692), and *Fame and Posthumous Works* (1700). This was no small achievement when one considers, as Asunción Lavrin has shown, the minimal publishing rate by women in the seventeenth century. Which does not mean that nuns in New Spain didn't write. On the contrary, they wrote at the instigation of their male superiors so as, in Lavrin's words, "to refine the self and ultimately achieve perfection," but never for sheer pleasure.

"*Abstention, mortification, renunciation,* and *humiliation* are all key words in the religious vocabulary of the colonial period," Lavrin states, and they color the legacy of these sisters. What makes Sor Juana stand out is her literary power, the subtlety of her subversion, and her pursuit of secular forms of knowledge. She was and was not a typical nun: she obeyed her superiors and performed her conventual duties, but at the same time, she didn't seem to have a clear sense of religious vocation, as most of her companions did. Sor Juana was a contemporary of other remarkable women, such as Sor Marcela de San Félix and sculptor Luisa Roldán of Spain, the Mesdames de Sevigne and de Lafayette of France, and Sor María de San José of colonial Mexico, a self-flagellating mystic who was requested by the bishop of Puebla to record her visions; but they were all exceptions to the norm.

To make a wide range of books a part of her being, to inhabit them, Sor Juana had to become an anomaly—in her own words, a rara avis. The *Response to Sor Filotea* is filled with delicious anecdotes about her love affair with books. "I was not yet three years old," she writes, "when my mother determined to send one of my elder sisters to learn to read at a school for girls. . . . Affection, and mischief, caused me to follow her, and when I observed how she was being taught her lessons I was so inflamed with the desire to know how to read, that deceiving—for so I knew it to be—the mistress, I told her that my mother had meant for me to have lessons too. She did not believe it, as it was little to be believed, but, to humor me, she acceded."

Sor Juana goes on to describe how she "abstained from eating cheese because I had heard that it made one slow of wits, for in me the desire for learning was stronger than the desire for eating." And she establishes a pattern when, sometime later, "being six or seven, and having learned how to read and write, along with all other skills of needlework and household arts that girls learn, it came to my attention that in Mexico City there were schools, and a University, in which one studied the sciences. The moment I heard this, I began to plague my mother with insistent and importunate pleas: she should dress me in a boy's clothing and send me to Mexico City to live with relatives, to study and be tutored at the University. She would not permit it."

The connection between her thirst for knowledge and her female body is quite strong. "I began to study Latin grammar . . . and so intense was my concern that though among women (especially a woman in the flower of her youth) the natural adornment of one's hair is held in such high esteem, I cut off mine to the breadth of some four to six fingers: measuring the place it had reached, and imposing upon myself the condition that if by the time it had again grown to that length I had not learned such and such a thing I had set for myself to learn while my hair was growing, I would again cut it off as punishment for being so slowwitted. And it did happen that my hair grew out and still I had not learned what I had set for myself—because my hair grew quickly and I learned slowly—and in fact I did cut it in punishment for such stupidity: for there seemed to me no cause for a head to be adorned with hair and naked of learning."

PHILOSOPHY OF THE KITCHEN

4

The precise circumstances of Sor Juana's birth are still somewhat obscure. She was born at the hacienda of San Miguel Nepantla, in the shadow of the volcano Popocatépetl, not far from what is today Mexico City, on either December 2, 1648, or November 12, 1651. Since Father Diego Calleja, her first biographer (or, better, hagiographer), a Jesuit and Sor Juana's contemporary who saw her life as an act of ascendancy, an allegory of sublime spirituality, introduced the latter date, it was accepted as correct for decades; but modern scholars have unraveled records that appear to establish her baptism three years earlier. Juana Ramírez de Asbaje was Sor Juana's given name.

Hers was a family of small landowners of modest means. What is certain is that, just like her two sisters, Sor Juana was a "natural" child—that is, born out of wedlock. How this fact marked her vision of the world and her standing in society is a controversial issue among sorjuanistas. Apparently she repeatedly tried to hide her illegitimacy. Several critics believed it was at the core of Sor Juana's existential dilemma and is the main reason for her becoming a nun. This might be an exaggeration, though. "Natural" children were common in New Spain, not only among the lower classes but among nuns and viceroys. (Fray Payo Enríquez de Rivera, aka don Payo, appointed viceroy of New Spain in 1674 and one of Sor Juana's protectors, was also illegitimate.) Not only could one find all sorts of ways to ameliorate the impact of one's "natural" birth, but the fact that this was a common occurrence reduced its stigmatization.

Sor Juana's father, Pedro Manuel de Asbaje, was a Basque frequently absent from the household. He goes unmentioned in the *Response to Sor Filotea*, which says something about the family dynamics. Sor Juana is absolutely silent about him, so many questions remain. Did she know him? Did they spend time together? Was he aware of his daughter's extraordinary talents, and did he encourage them? Paz suggests the possibility that Sor Juana was the daughter of a certain Friar F. (or H.) de Asvaje, but this is unlikely. In any event, the enigma of the paternal figure is central, not only to her life but to the Mexican psyche. Since the arrival of Hernán Cortés, the father figure has been portrayed as an intruder, a foreigner—the Spanish conquistador interested in gold and power, promiscuous and irresponsible, who propagated the mestizo race. The fact that we know so little about Pedro Manuel de Asbaje has helped turn the model of Sor Juana, the bastard child, into an archetype of the collective Mexican soul.

As for Sor Juana's mother, Isabel Ramírez: she was a criolla who seems to have been the center of gravity in her daughter's life. It appears that in the absence of the children's father, she took control of the hacienda in Nepantla, and her strong character kept the family afloat. Sor Juana's love for her is clear in the way she wanted to be known publicly almost as soon as she began writing poetry: as Juana Ramírez de Asbaje, with her mother's family name first. She seems to have written about her mother regularly; anecdotes and references to her appear in the *Response to Sor Filotea*, in her plays, and in her poetry, testimony, no doubt, to the respect and appreciation she carried with her always.

Brilliant and precocious even as a young girl, Sor Juana found refuge and fulfillment in the library of her grandfather, Pedro Ramírez. At eight she wrote a poem about the Eucharist for a religious festival. She had some Latin lessons, but since her formal education ended at the primary level, most of her learning came from her reading.

Associating Sor Juana with the kitchen is a common trope in her stubborn popularity. This isn't unexpected. In spite of the rapid changes brought along by modernity, women in Mexico are still perceived as being in charge of the culinary domain. There is a somewhat deceiving book, called *Las recetas de cocina de Sor Juana* (2001), showcasing an assortment of recipes. They include *buñuelos de queso, torta de arroz, guisado prieto, pudín de espinaca, mancha manteles,* and *pollas portuguesas.* Truth is, none appear in her *Obra completa* (1951), edited by Alfonso Méndez Plancarte and Alberto C. Salceda. It is likely that these recipes came from the Convento de San Jerónimo, which since 1979 has housed the Universidad del Claustro de Sor Juana, in Mexico City's downtown. Sor Juana's popularity was used as a ploy to sell the recipes as her own concoctions.

Still, the kitchen does feature in her *Response to Sor Filotea.* "What shall I tell you, lady, of the natural secrets I have discovered while cooking?" she wrote. "I see that an egg holds together and fries in butter or in oil, but, on the contrary, in syrup shrivels into shreds; observe that to keep sugar in a liquid state one need only add a drop or two of water in which a quince or other bitter fruit has been soaked; observe that the yolk and the white of one egg are so dissimilar that each with sugar produces a result not obtainable with both together. I do not wish to weary you with such inconsequential matters, and make mention of them only to give you full notice of my nature. . . . What wisdom may be ours if not the philosophies of the kitchen? . . . Had Aristotle prepared victuals, he would have written more."

The lesson one learns from Sor Juana's connection to the kitchen is that it is a laboratory of study. In describing it, she might have been visualizing an alchemist's workroom, which hasn't stopped representations of her in the kitchen with more explicit messages. At times she is labeled a seducer using her ingredients to plot a certain liaison, while in other depictions the nun is seen as a protoscientist experimenting with the elements.

5

A DOUBLE HANDICAP

The world into which Sor Juana was thrown was obsessed with, and nervous about, race and identity. As a colony, the seventeenth-century viceroyalty of New Spain was totally dependent on the Spanish Crown. Colonial governmental autonomy was minimal, and culture, as well, moved from west to east: society was organized hierarchically, on the basis of race and birthright. The role of El Santo Oficio, the Holy Office of the Inquisition, was that of a brutal police force: it preserved the considerable gap between one group and another by calling attention to an individual's honor and publicly castigating those falsifying an ethnic identity.

Since the Reconquista of the Iberian Peninsula at the end of the fifteenth century, the concept of *pureza de sangre*, purity of blood, had colored every aspect of life, from food and medicine to diplomacy and the arts. It justified the expulsion of Moors and Jews from Spanish territory by legitimizing the lineage of the *cristianos viejos*, old Christians, and opened up an acerbic debate around the notion of *el honor*, an individual's honor and moral standing.

This racial craze was at the heart of the colonizing enterprise in the Americas, built on the basis of transculturation. The Spaniards had encountered a strong indigenous population and quickly established a system of castes. At the top of the ladder were the ruling *españoles*, Spanish settlers heading legal and financial institutions. Next came the *criollos*, American-born descendants of the Spaniards. They were followed by the part-European and part-native *mestizos*, and then by the *castizos*, whose heritage was *mestizo* and white. The *indios* were next, and at the bottom of the ladder were *mulatos, zambos,* and other ethnic mixtures of Indians and African slaves.

The divisions were not limited to race. Gender played as important a role as skin color in the shaping of society and its world view. Male rule prevailed, a direct result of the male composition of the army led by Hernán Cortés. Unlike their counterparts in the British colonies to the north, the Iberian *conquistadores* crossed the Atlantic without spouses. Their goal was not to start from scratch to build an altogether new civilization, to become the new people of Israel in search of a New Canaan this side of the Atlantic. Instead, their objective was encapsulated in the words *oro* and *poder,* "gold" and "power." Their mandate was to subdue the native population and build a dependency whose riches the Spanish Catholic monarchs could use to enhance their domain. Leaving their female companions behind in Europe allowed them to be free, to seek and possess pleasure.

In Sor Juana's time, women were restricted to three milieus: the domestic, the courtly, and the monastic. All were male dominated, and the role handed down to the women varied from realm to realm: in the privacy of the homestead, wives were expected to be passive and caring; in the flamboyant corridors of the court, women were objects of adoration; and in the cloister, nuns were silent and contemplative observers. These set social patterns made it difficult for a talented young girl, a hybrid of Spaniard and criolla, to live freely without attracting suspicion. Still, Sor Juana managed to move in circles of power, meeting important government and church officials, seeking the security of their protection while launching a career as an intellectual that would take her far beyond the limits they set.

Identity was at the core of Sor Juana's personal quest. She understood early on that to excel she would need to arm herself with a sense of security and self-esteem that precluded all possible doubts about her character. "One truth I shall not deny," she writes in the *Response to Sor Filotea,* "(first, because it is well-known to all, and second, because although it has not worked in my favor, God has granted me the mercy of loving truth above all else), which is that from the moment I was first illuminated by the light of reason, my inclination towards letters has been so vehement, so overpowering, that not even the admonitions of others—and I have suffered many—nor my own meditations—and they have not been few—have been sufficient to cause me to forswear this natural impulse that God placed in me."

And the admonitions were indeed many. Her autobiographical letters enumerate the countless obstacles placed before her. But giving up was not an option. She was a woman born out of wedlock, a double handicap, but perhaps she could turn it to her advantage if her achievements could overwhelm her critics. Appearances, contrived and authentic—a favorite Baroque theme in the Spanish Golden Age—are the vertebrae unifying her entire body of work. Her poems deal with hypocrisy and pretense, with mirrors and original models, with the shallowness of social behavior and the vulnerability of women to male demands.

Her cloak-and-dagger 1683 comedy *The Trials of a Noble House* and her mythological love-intrigue play *Love Is a Greater Labyrinth* deal with the confusing effects of choice. Unlike those Iberian dramatists she clearly imitated (Lope de Vega, Tirso de Molina, Calderón de la Barca, and others), she wrote not for the public stage but for the palace—that is, for an aristocratic audience—and her dramas offer no clear solutions to the mysteries of identity.

There is little extant information about Sor Juana's entrance to the viceregal court. Her *Response to Sor Filotea* jumps abruptly from her childhood to her convent life, leaving the years in between— roughly from 1656, when her grandfather died, to 1669, when she entered the convent—in the dark. Her biographers have thus been forced to speculate, to fill in the gaps by way of inference. We know that while she was still at home, a new lover, Diego Ruíz Lozano, came into her mother's life. Then, at age thirteen, Sor Juana moved to the capital, into the house of a wealthy uncle and aunt, don Juan de Mata and doña María Ramírez, who presented her at the viceregal court. Father Calleja observes that the urban elite were immediately entranced by her. Her cleverness, intelligence, and beauty made her an instant sensation. In 1664, after eight years with her relatives, she met the newly arrived vicereine, doña Leonor Carreto, Marquesa de Mancera, who quickly admitted Sor Juana to her service.

In hindsight, the double handicap might have served as traction for Sor Juana. A limitation might be an excuse to be daring, a way to justify one's courage. It might have galvanized her. Under such restrictions, what was there to lose?

6

LESBIAN LOVE?

Judging by the sonnets, *décimas*, *seguidillas*, epigrams, *redondillas*, *romances*, and other poetry Sor Juana produced, she was fascinated by the flirtations, the sensuous codes, and the secret provocations of courtly manners. But life at court was not pure leisure, and her duties were fixed: she would be both companion and confidante to her patrons and write under their commission in exchange for a routine that allowed her to cultivate her intellectual interests and escape marital responsibilities.

Some of her poetry written under the patronage of various vicereines is intense, candid, burning with passion, qualities that have invited speculation: was she sentimentally involved with some of these women? Her loyalty and gratitude to the Marquesa de Mancera, known as "Laura" in her work, is expressed in three funerary sonnets on the marquesa's death, in which Sor Juana thanks her patroness for encouraging and supporting her poetic drive. According to historical data, the Marquesa de Mancera was around thirty years of age when the two women met.

Father Calleja believes the marquesa "could not live without her servant," and Paz describes their liaison as "a composite of selfishness and admiration, sympathy and pity . . . a relationship of superior to inferior, of protectress to protegee, but one in which there was also recognition of an exceptional young woman's worth." Sor Juana also had relationships with three viceroys: Fray Payo de Rivera; don Tomás Antonio de la Cerda, the Marqués de la Laguna; and don Gaspar de la Cerda Silva Sandoval y Mendoza, the Conde de Galve, whose wife was the subject of a set of poems Sor Juana wrote between 1688 and the time of her death.

Of all of her patronesses, María Luisa Manrique de Lara y Gonzaga, Condesa de Paredes and Marquesa de la Laguna, known as "Lysis" in Sor Juana's writing, was probably the dearest. Their friendship was colored by tacit eroticism, as is clear in the poems written in the condesa's honor between 1680 and 1685, three of which (*décimas* 126, 130, and 132) are included in the modern edition of Sor Juana's *Complete Works*, edited by Méndez Plancarte and Salceda. Intelligent, energetic, and extremely beautiful, the Condesa de Paredes encouraged Sor Juana to compose what some consider her best work, *The Divine Narcissus*, a sacramental play full of allegorical references, possibly written in 1688.

The subject matter of its *loa*, a small dramatic scene that serves as an introduction and is often performed on its own, is of great importance: the Indian population in New Spain and the birth of a new civilization. The main characters are Occident, personified by a stately Indian wearing a crown, and America, a noble Indian woman. Together with her friend and devotee Carlos de Sigüenza y Góngora, Mexico's leading man of letters in the seventeenth century, who in 1668 wrote *Primavera indiana*, a long poem in honor of the Virgen de Guadalupe, Sor Juana was among the first to juxtapose Christianity and native pagan mythology and to reflect on the encounter between the two civilizations. The loa is structured as a debate between European monotheism and Aztec idolatry; although the character representing idolatry refuses to accept the Christian doctrine, by the end it understands, in a syncretistic view, that the faiths have much in common.

The Condesa de Paredes also helped Sor Juana pay for her first published collection of poems: *Castalian Inundation*, which appeared in Madrid and was dedicated to her patroness. Did they share a lesbian love? Should we consider the risks Sor Juana took in her poems as a token of gratitude and affection typical of the time? The answers to these questions are elusive. They have generated bewilderment and confusion among cultural historians and biographers, some of whom are ready to venture risky hypotheses whereas others prefer a more conservative, less speculative stance.

For instance, María Luisa Bemberg's film *I, the Worst of All* (1990), with Dominique Sanda and Assumpta Serna and inspired by Paz's *The Traps of Faith*, underscores erotic elements in their relationship by having the condesa visit Sor Juana's convent cell, ask her to uncover her hair, and eventually kiss her on the mouth. That such an encounter took place is highly improbable. It is true that there was a constant flow of gifts between the viceregal palace and the Convent of Santa Paula. Furthermore, the condesa is known to have paid innumerable visits to Sor Juana. But strict rules forbade visitors, no matter how powerful and well connected they were, to enter a nun's cell, let alone engage in physical love with her.

And there is a Netflix miniseries, *Juana Inés* (2016), created by Patricia Arriaga Jordán and starring Arcelia Ramírez, Yolanda Corrales, and Hernán del Riego, targeting a trans-Hispanic audience, that delves into this dimension. Sor Juana's lesbian self is similar to Frida Kahlo's bisexuality: at a time of gender reconsideration, it becomes an apparently forbidden topic everyone indulges in. In Sor Juana's case, the topic has been a favorite of Chicanas, who during the civil rights era embraced the Virgin of Guadalupe, Sor Juana, and lesbianism as symbols of change. It appears in Yolanda M. López's pictorial art and in Alicia Gaspar de Alba's novel *Sor Juana's Second Dream* (1999).

Indeed, explicit images of Sor Juana's purported lesbianism abound. There are also depictions of her with an upraised fist. And, along the same lines, altars and representations of her as a fashionable *feminista*.

Is it really feminism, though? We are talking about a movement that, with a clear ideological drive, acquires momentum in the nineteenth century around the issue of women's suffrage but doesn't become a capstone endeavor until the mid-twentieth century, when in the French-speaking world Simone de Beauvoir publishes *Le deuxième sexe* (1949) and in the English-speaking world Betty Friedan writes *The Feminine Mystique* (1969), inspiring a plan of action to change the cultural perception of women in Western civilization.

Should Sor Juana be described as a precursor of the movement—a protofeminist—that many centuries before?

When Octavio Paz published his canonical biography *The Traps of Faith*, he was rightfully criticized for looking at her femininity with surgical eyes. For him, Sor Juana was a poet who as a woman understood the conundrum of her sex in colonial Mexico. But hers wasn't a political voice, at least not overtly. Paz praised her refined taste, her capacity to be blunt without being radical.

To Paz's critics, he missed the whole picture. In their opinion, she was a radical. Never dogmatic, she was ready to sacrifice everything, including her own voice, to advance the cause of women. For that, she paid a heavy price. As such, she became a martyr. The Danish existentialist philosopher Søren Kierkegaard said the difference between a tyrant and a martyr is that when the former dies, his rule is over, whereas when the latter dies, her rule begins.

At any rate, this embrace—Sor Juana as spokesperson *avant la lettre*—comes with a twist. Feminism in the United States, even among Latinos, is, on the surface, more outspoken than in Latin America. A recurrent critique of the Chicano movement is that, although it pushed labor improvement for Mexican migrant workers while opening its wings to other similar causes, in the end the machismo at its core was utterly destructive. With the exception of Dolores Huerta, the Chicano leaders—from Cesar Chavez to Reies López Tijerina, Rodolfo "Corky" González, and others—established an ideological paradigm defined by their male world view. The uses of Sor Juana weren't only against the white establishment but inside the movement as well.

Another important dimension of this iconographic aspect of Sor Juana is that Mexico might be seen as lagging behind the United States in terms of gender equality, yet as a woman Sor Juana has been featured in the nation's currency. Gay marriage was accepted in Mexico before it was in the United States. And Mexico, in its history, has had far more female political leaders—congressional representatives, senators, and others—than its neighbor to the north. Perhaps Sor Juana is more than an inspiration: in Mexico, she may be an engine of change.

7

SOR
JUANA
INES
DE LA
CRUZ

"YOU HAVE COMPELLED ME"

JUSTICE

KarlyCherry

Sor Juana wrote most of her poetry after she took the veil. For her nonreligious stanzas, she always drew on her life at court. Is she exaggerating when she states in the *Response to Sor Filotea* that "I have never written on my own choice, but at the urging of others, to whom with reason I might say, *You have compelled me*"? Similarly, she claims, in *A Spiritual Self-Defense*, "I have extremely resisted in writing [the miserable verses] and have excused myself in every possible way." Almost everything she wrote, with the exception of "El sueño," was commissioned by, and dedicated to, important personalities of her time, not only patrons.

Between 1671 and 1680, she composed a couple of *romances* to don Payo; she also wrote homages to the Duque de Veraguas, her Latin teacher Martín de Olivas, Kings Philip IV and Charles II, and Sigüenza y Góngora. A selection from *Castalian Inundation* illustrates her style and themes. It opens with three examples of the *romance*, a simple and widely used Spanish ballad written in octosyllabic verse in which the even-numbered lines rhyme with the same assonance and the odd-numbered lines are left free.

"Prologue to the Reader," with which Sor Juana begins her first book of poetry, is a standard introduction filled with a modesty customary in her time but absurd in ours: she offers her poems with a de rigueur sense of hesitation, "though all that may speak well of them / . . . I know them to be poor." "In Reply to a Gentleman from Peru," another invaluable document on her status as a woman in colonial Mexico, is an epistolary *romance* addressed to a certain señor Navarrete, who sent Sor Juana a set of clay vessels from Chile and some original poems in which, by way of commending her, he suggested "she would better be a man." Her response is a brief manifesto on the value of women's roles as pleasure objects and wives, neither of which she accepts for herself. It is also an forceful yet implicit confession of sexual identity. She posits:

> Con que a mí no es bien mirado
> que como a una mujer me miren,
> pues no soy mujer que a alguno
> de mujer pueda servirle;
> y sólo sé que mi cuerpo,
> sin que a uno u otro se incline,
> es neutro, o abstracto, cuanto
> sólo el Alma deposite.

My English translation:

> So in my case, it is looked down
> for me to be seen as woman,
> for a woman I shall never be
> who may as woman serve a man;
> and I know only that my body,
> not inclined to one or other,
> is neutral, or abstract, to
> what only the Soul consigns.

The third *romance*, "While by Grace I am inspired," has a sacred theme. Included in volume 3 of the edition by Méndez Plancarte, it chronicles the ongoing antagonism between faith and reason, neither of which can cure the suffering of her soul. The dichotomy in this poem can serve to underscore the main motifs of *el barroco hispano*, a Baroque style in fashion in the Spanish Golden Age until roughly

1680, the latest date of Calderón de la Barca's *autos*, and, with renewed intensity in the New World, from early colonial times through the age of independence in the early eighteenth century and onward into the present. Its prime objective is to call attention to the artificiality of human endeavors by accentuating their unnatural character.

Baroque art abounds in conceits and counterfeits, in theatricality and obsessive sophistication, to the extent that, as Borges once put it, these endeavors "run the risk of becoming caricatures of themselves." In Baroque poetry, verbal puns are ever present, designed to call attention to the fragile line between reality and fantasy, between beauty and ugliness, and, as in Sor Juana's *romance*, between faith and reason. Why *lo barroco*, although practiced all over Europe from 1580 on, ended up becoming a signature of Hispanic American culture at large is still a subject of heated debate. Such a style is likely to flourish in environments where a variety of diverse, often antagonistic ethnic, linguistic, and religious backgrounds clash, generating a state of impurity and contamination, an atmosphere of hybridization like that found on the Iberian Peninsula after the expulsion of the Jews in 1492.

In the Americas, the mingling of various backgrounds—Indian, Iberian, and African—resulted in what the Cuban ethnographer Fernando Ortíz once called "a transcultural milieu." But other factors also contributed to the reign of *lo barroco* in Spain and its dissemination in the colonies across the Atlantic: the struggle between Reformation and Counter-Reformation, the defeat of the Spanish Armada, and the crisis of Catholicism.

Baroque Spanish poetry developed two alternative modes: the *culteranismo* of Luis de Góngora y Argote (1561–1627), infatuated with learned words and a labyrinthine syntax, and the *conceptismo* of Francisco Gómez de Quevedo y Villegas (1580–1645), characterized by ingenious conceits. Whereas the former embellishes by means of verbal pyrotechnics, the latter makes poetry an instrument for investigating existential dilemmas. In New Spain, where the Spanish Baroque was taken to its limits, Góngora was seen as the more admirable of the two, but Quevedo was also influential, as were Lope de Vega, Calderón de la Barca, and Baltasar Gracián.

Probably nobody has studied these links with the vision and perseverance of Octavio Paz, who in 1958 compiled an important anthology, *Mexican Poetry*, which includes many well- and lesser-known literary figures of colonial Mexico, such as Francisco de Terrazas, Bernardo de Balbuena, Juan Ruíz de Alarcón, Miguel de Guevara, and Luis de Sandoval y Zapata. (Intriguingly, in its English-language incarnation the anthology was translated by none other than Samuel Beckett, whose knowledge of the Spanish language was limited. Yet the renditions are superb.) In *The Traps of Faith*, Paz places them in context. "It has often been said—both in praise and deprecation—that the Mexican baroque was an exaggeration of the Spanish models," he observes. "Indeed, like all imitative art, the poetry of New Spain attempted to surpass its models: it was the extreme of baroqueness, the apogee of strangeness. This excess is proof of its authenticity."

Nevertheless, amid this strangeness, Sor Juana has a room of her own: her Baroque voice is neither misguided nor excessive, and by virtue of her status as a colonial woman, the dichotomies she writes of in *romances* like "While by Grace, I am inspired" and sonnets such as "In my pursuit, World, why such diligence?" possess an urgency no Spanish poet could dream of. That urgency is particularly tangible in "Detente, sombra" (in English, "Stay, shadow"). It is difficult to come up with a more commanding, more eloquent poem about the inter-section between imagination and desire. This is the Spanish original, followed by my English translation:

> Detente, sombra de mi bien esquivo
> imagen del hechizo que más quiero,
> bella ilusión por quien alegre muero,
> dulce ficción por quien penosa vivo.
> Si al imán de tus gracias atractivo
> sirve mi pecho de obediente acero,
> ¿para qué me enamoras lisonjero,
> si has de burlarme luego fugitivo?
> Mas blasonar no puedes satisfecho
> de que triunfa de mí tu tiranía;
> que aunque dejas burlado el lazo estrecho
> que tu forma fantástica ceñía,
> poco importa burlar brazos y pecho
> si te labra prisión mi fantasía.

Stay, shadow of my elusive prize
image of enchantment I most want,
fair illusion for whom I joyfully die,
sweet fiction for whom I painfully live.
If to the magnet of your charm's attraction
serves my breast of obedient steel,
why do you entice me with your flattery,
if you then will fool me with escape?
'Tis you can't boast in satisfaction
that I fell victim to your tyranny;
though while you fooled the straight bond
that your fantastic form constrained,
it matters little to fool arms and breast
if my fantasy holds you prisoner.

By definition, all of Latin American literature written in the Spanish language is derivative: Spanish is a foreign artifact adapted to native needs, an import, a hand-me-down. But Sor Juana, much like Borges nearly three centuries later, found originality in imitation. While Góngora's fingerprints and a certain Quevedian mood lurk in many corners of her work, she is never so derivative as to lose her own personality. What distinguishes her from the Spanish masters is her political agenda: not only is she a poet, but she is a female poet; not only is she a Catholic, but she is a Catholic nun living under strict male rule within the confines of the church in New Spain; not only is she infatuated with neologisms and other precious words, but she uses them to call attention to the artificiality of the Spanish language in the colonies, where all sonnets are echoes of other sonnets.

In short, Sor Juana is wise enough to turn her status as a colonial woman poet to her advantage: if she is derivative, it is because she must depend on others. And she did more than incorporate Mexican motifs into her writings. She was also among the first to experiment with Nahuatl ballads, known as *tocotines*, traditional Indian-style dance songs of which she wrote two. One mixes Nahuatl and Spanish; the other, composed in 1676, is in Nahuatl in its entirety. Its subject is the Assumption of the Virgin; it makes fun of the way blacks and Indians react to the ascension of the Virgen de Guadalupe. This poem is of enormous relevance. Dependent as it was on Europe, the criollo

intelligentsia of seventeenth-century New Spain denigrated indigenous folklore. But Sor Juana's scope was much larger: in her work one
witnesses the metamorphosis of the poetry of New Spain into the
poetry of Mexico.

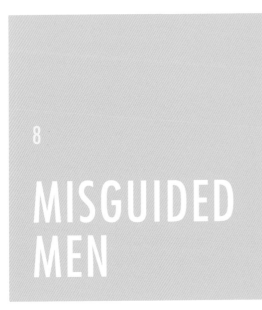

8

MISGUIDED MEN

Sor Juana's overall ideological stance is nowhere clearer than in her philosophical satire "Hombres necios" (in English, "Stubborn men"):

Hombres necios que acusáis
a la mujer sin razón,
sin ver que sois la ocasión
de lo mismo que culpáis:

si con ansia sin igual
solicitáis su desdén,
¿por qué queréis que obren bien
si las incitáis al mal?

Combatís su resistencia
y luego, con gravedad,
decís que fue liviandad
lo que hizo la diligencia.

Parecer quiere el denuedo
de vuestro parecer loco,

al niño que pone el coco
y luego le tiene miedo.

Queréis, con presunción necia,
hallar a la que buscáis,
para pretendida, Thais,
y en la posesión, Lucrecia.

¿Qué humor puede ser más raro
que el que, falto de consejo,
él mismo empaña el espejo,
y siente que no esté claro?

Con el favor y el desdén
tenéis condición igual,
quejándoos, si os tratan mal,
burlándoos, si os quieren bien.

Opinión, ninguna gana;
pues la que más se recata,
si no os admite, es ingrata,
y si os admite, es liviana.

Siempre tan necios andáis
que, con desigual nivel,
a una culpáis por cruel
y a otra por fácil culpáis.

¿Pues cómo ha de ser templada
la que vuestro amor pretende,
si la que es ingrata, ofende,
y la que es fácil, enfada?

Mas, entre el enfado y pena
que vuestro gusto refiere,
bien haya la que no os quiere
y quejaos en hora buena.

Dan vuestras amantes penas
a sus libertades alas,
y después de hacerlas malas
las queréis hallar muy buenas.

¿Cuál mayor culpa ha tenido
en una pasión errada:
la que cae de rogada,
o el que ruega de caído?

¿O cuál es más de culpar,
aunque cualquiera mal haga:
la que peca por la paga,
o el que paga por pecar?

Pues ¿para qué os espantáis
de la culpa que tenéis?
Queredlas cual las hacéis
o hacedlas cual las buscáis.

Dejad de solicitar,
y después, con más razón,
acusaréis la afición
de la que os fuere a rogar.

Bien con muchas armas fundo
que lidia vuestra arrogancia,
pues en promesa e instancia
juntáis diablo, carne y mundo.

My English version:

Stubborn men, who will chastise
a woman without cause,
oblivious that you're the source
of what you've criticized;

if your passion is so strong

that you elicit their disdain,
why do you wish they restrain
when you incite them to wrong?

You topple their defense,
and then, with gravity,
you credit sensuality
for what was won with diligence.

Your daring must be confronted,
for your sense is no less bogus
than the child who fears the ogre,
then weeps when is revolted.

Your presumptions are bound,
that for a wife you want Lucrece,
in lovers you prefer Thaïs,
thus seeking blessings be found.

What humor brings more fear,
which, without counsel to be found,
itself first the mirror ground
then lament it isn't clear?

With either favor or disdain
the selfsame purpose you achieve,
if they love, they are deceived,
if they don't, then you complain.

No woman will suit your taste
with circumspection as virtue:
ungrateful, she who love you not,
yet she who does, she's a waste.

You men are such stubborn breed,
appraised with ungodly rule,
the first you charge with being cruel,
the second, easy, you feed.

How might she bring you gains,
the one with love to extend?
If not willing, she'll offend,
and if willing, she inflames.

Amid anger and torment
your whimsy results in flair,
one is found who doesn't care:
then quickly your grievances vent.

So lovingly you bring her pain
that inhibitions run in fray;
why, after leading them astray,
should you wish without strain?

Who will greater guilt incur
when is passion that's misleading?
She who errs and heeds his pleading,
or he who pleads for her to err?

Who's is greater guilt therein
when all conduct will dismay:
she who sins and takes the pay,
or he who hires her to sin?

Why, for sins you're guilty of
do you still your blame debate?
Either love what you create
or create what you might love.

Were it not better to abstain,
and so, with finer stimulation,
obtain unforced admiration
of her you plotted to contain?

In such landscape to behold,
with your arms and arrogance,
in promise and deliverance
adjoin devil, flesh, and world.

In this, Sor Juana's most famous *redondilla*, she delivers an indictment that goes beyond class lines, criticizing men for manipulating women and reprimanding women for their passivity and submission to men. She includes references to Thaïs, the Athenian mistress of Alexander the Great and Ptolemy and known as a symbol of liberalism; and to Lucretia, a Roman exemplar of "the virtuous wife," who, raped and betrayed by the son of Tarquin the Proud, ultimately committed suicide. Shaped as a Spanish stanza in octosyllabic quatrains rhymed *abba*, it is even today memorized in part by schoolchildren in Mexico and throughout Latin America who grasp only a fragment of its overall meaning and hence simplify the poetess's message. Its popularity might well be based, as Electa Arenal and Amanda Powell claim, on "the suppressed anger it reveals in women and the giddy catharsis it permits men."

This *redondilla* is both endearing and accessible, at least when one compares it to Sor Juana's epigrams and *décimas*, stanzas of ten octosyllabic lines with a rhyme scheme of *abbaabbacdc*, and, particularly, to her sonnets with an Italianate rhyme scheme. In the sonnets her talent is at its apex: she displays a perfect grasp of her themes as well as astonishing stylistic control. Those qualities are best appreciated in classic examples such as "This that you gaze on, colorful deceit," "In my pursuit, World, why such diligence?," and "Stay, shadow of contentment too short-lived." They have recurrent themes: love and indiscretion, individual honor, and, her favorite dichotomy, female vanity versus female intellect.

The scope of her register affirms her versatility and genius, but she was comfortable in other literary forms and wrote medleys, panegyrics, devotional exercises, riddles for parlor guessing games, even a treatise on musical methods (now lost), entitled *The Conch Shell*. One could ascribe to Sor Juana a psychological urgency to excel against all odds. Her road to success was blocked by obstacles, not the least of which was her gender. Father Aguiar y Seijas, the archbishop of Mexico, disliked her to such a degree that after she died, he confiscated her belongings and fought to erase her from human memory. Father Aguiar y Seijas had arranged for the publication in Mexico of Father Vieyra's sermon and so may have taken Sor Juana's critique of it as an indirect attack on himself.

Sor Juana's willingness to face the likes of the archbishop shows how courageous she was, how she needed to test herself constantly, to surpass her male competitors, to call attention to their mediocrity and signal their shortcomings. Since her achievements generated envy, she handled herself with discretion, scattering clues to her existential dilemma in various parts of her oeuvre. One such clue is the famous monologue of doña Leonor, a young woman trapped at the crossroads where female beauty and intellectual talents meet, in the play *The Trials of a Noble House*. In act I, scene II, doña Leonor tells her confidantes doña Ana and Cecilia:

> Decirte que nací hermosa
> presumo que es excusado,
> pues lo atestiguan tus ojos
> y lo prueban mis trabajos.
> Sólo diré . . . Aquí quisiera
> no ser yo quien lo relato,
> pues en callarlo o decirlo
> dos inconvenientes hallo:
> porque si digo que fui
> celebrada por milagros
> de discreción, me desmiente
> la necesidad de contarlo;
> y si lo callo, no informo
> de mí, y en un mismo caso
> me desmiento si lo afirmo,
> y lo ignoras si lo callo.

My English translation:

> To tell you I was born beautiful
> I assume is excused,
> since your eyes shall bear witness
> and my labors are proof.
> I shall say . . . Here I wouldn't want
> to be telling the story,
> since in telling it or be silent
> two inconveniences I find:
> since if I say I was
> celebrated for miracles

of discretion, I disproved
by the need to narrate;
and since if I am silent, none
will know the truth, and so,
I betray myself if I speak,
and you'll ignore me if I don't.

And a few lines later:

Era de mi patria toda
el objeto venerado
de aquellas adoraciones
que forma el común aplauso;
y como lo que decía
fuese bueno o fuese malo,
ni el rostro lo deslucía,
ni lo desairaba el garbo,
llegó la superstición
popular a empeño tanto
que yo adoraba deidad
el ídolo que formaron.

I was in my native land
a venerated object
of adorations formed
by common applause;
and since whatever I said
was either good or bad,
either by gesture caught,
or by demeanor found,
popular superstition was
that I became an adored deity
people had idolized.

Sor Juana's life and career drastically changed in 1669, when all of a sudden, after enjoying enormous success in the viceregal court, she chose the contemplative environment of the convent. She gave up earthly pleasures for a life of meditation. The transformation was stunning: she switched identities; she became somebody altogether different. The metamorphosis began with changing her name: she ceased to be Juana Ramírez de Asbaje and became Sor Juana Inés de la Cruz, and, by virtue of her talents, was nicknamed by her contemporaries, as mentioned before, "the Tenth Muse" and "the Mexican Phoenix."

First she joined a convent of the Barefoot Carmelites, but after three months she found the regimen too dogmatic, too strict. After a brief return to her life at court, she finally joined the more liberal Convent of Santa Paula, where she would stay for her remaining twenty-six years.

9

"REPUGNANT TO MY NATURE"

This decision by Sor Juana is also surrounded by mystery. "And so I entered the religious order," she writes in her *Response to Sor Filotea*, "knowing that life there entailed certain conditions (I refer to superficial, and not fundamental, regards) most repugnant to my nature; but given the antipathy I felt for marriage, I deemed convent life the least unsuitable and the most honorable I could elect if I were to insure my salvation." But why did she quit the comfort of aristocratic circles so abruptly? Why become a nun? Was her faith strong enough to handle a daily routine of prayer and devotion? Or was she running away from scandal? Was a love affair the reason behind her escape? Sor Juana might have seen marriage as the expected objective of her period at court and wanted to escape it; she might have begun to perceive the court as too frivolous an atmosphere for serious thinking; and she might simply have imagined the reclusiveness of nuns as the best context in which to pursue her intellectual quest.

Mexico City had some twenty-nine religious institutions for nuns at the end of the seventeenth century. They were semiautonomous and self-sufficient, dependent on the support of a centralized ecclesiastical organization, and survived by means of educational as well as agricultural and commercial activities. Many of these convents ran girls' schools, hospitals, and orphanages. Young daughters, brought by their fathers, took refuge in them from the responsibilities of society. Every act, though, came under male supervision. Enraptured by the voice of Christ, nuns were often forced by their confessors to write down these blissful communications.

Entering one of these convents wasn't easy: a dowry and proof of genealogical purity were required. The latter condition perhaps explains why, when Sor Juana entered Santa Paula, she falsified her background by declaring herself legitimate; otherwise, despite her reputation, she would have been rejected. A hierarchical structure organized different types of nuns according to their mystical elevation, degree of devotion, and administrative responsibilities. The Convent of Santa Paula had a girls' school that offered music, dance, and theater classes, in which Sor Juana participated by writing lyrics. Nuns were expected to follow a strict schedule of meals and prayers, but they joined in all sorts of activities, such as poetry tournaments, musical concerts, theatrical events, masquerades, and other happenings. On occasion lay visitors were allowed in, even invited to participate in conventual convocations, but only in restricted areas.

As critic Luis Harss states in *Sor Juana's Dream* (1986), "It was an age of great pageantry, given to grand entries through ceremonial arches, majestic *Te Deums* with ringing church bells, allegorical floats and fireworks, dramatic mystery plays, rousing popular farces. Although the conventual ideal was still sacrificial self-denial, many nuns, like vestal courtesans, led quite luxurious lives, with slaves and servants. They dressed in finery, wore jewelry, enjoyed comfortable furniture, and collected valuable ornaments."

The Convent of Santa Paula was founded in 1586 by a nun from the Royal Convent of the Immaculate Conception. It was intended only for criolla women. There Sor Juana led a rather comfortable life, unlike anything modern readers might visualize when invoking images of flagellant nuns in states of mystical ecstasy. Her cell was a large apartment with a sitting room and kitchen. Given considerable space for books, musical instruments, maps, and other research materials, she frequently found herself surrounded by the silence and tranquility conducive to writing at her leisure. She had other conveniences as well, including part-time domestic help—a servant to wash, cook, and attend to her earthly needs. A wealthy benefactor had endowed her with enough money to carry on a luxurious existence, and, judging by the accounts of her possessions, she amassed a distinguished collection of indigenous musical and scientific instruments, folk art, and other paraphernalia.

Like other nuns, Sor Juana was forbidden to leave Santa Paula's four walls, but through her reading and artistic endeavors she was able to travel in her imagination to distant places and to seek knowledge well beyond the confines of the convent, which she often found suffocating. She served as the convent's accountant, an elective position. Her relationships with various authorities within and outside the institution, mainly men, had many ups and downs: at one point, she was forced by the prioress, in response to Father Aguiar y Seijas, to abandon her studies for several months; and she was also tormented by Father Núñez de Miranda, her confessor, who constantly cautioned her against "sacrilegious paths."

Overall, the convent period was the most productive of Sor Juana's career. She was prolific, versatile, and challenging as a poet. Her thirst for knowledge was insatiable. "I myself can affirm," she wrote in the *Response to Sor Filotea*, "that what I have not understood in an author in one branch of knowledge I may understand in a second in a branch that seems remote from the first." She also was guileful, retaining her ties to the viceregal court in spite of the changing political climate.

A sign of her status and influence was the commission she received in 1680 to write a poem celebrating a triumphal cathedral arch to honor the advent of a new viceregal period, that of the Marqués de la Laguna. Sor Juana composed "Allegorical Neptune" as a dedication to the architectural structure and an explanation of its allusions, which included the figure of Neptune as a reference to the marqués. The poem itself is a web of biblical and mythological references, all of which reflect the defiant idea that male power depends on female wisdom.

Such works were a source of both pride and nervousness; they kept her in the public eye. And there is the question of her faith: as seen in her *romance* "While by Grace I am inspired," belief in Christ generated suffering and confusion within her, and this hint of skepticism would increase, and be fought against, as her years in Santa Paula went on. She would fight not to be perceived as superior to the other nuns and would visit them to comfort them, to discuss their pain, to be helpful. At the same time, though, she was quite aware that her fame and privileged position made her a target of animosity and envy, both within and without the convent, from those who, in her own words, "abhor one who excels." This led her more than once to compare her fate to that of Jesus persecuted by the Pharisees.

Proud of her body of work, she made sure no stanza of hers was "unbecoming." But only a single poem made her truly proud, "a little trifle . . . called 'El Sueño,'" which stands as her most astonishing creation. Written around 1685, this long epistemological poem is Sor Juana's most intellectually challenging legacy. Also known as "Primero sueño" (First Dream), it comprises 975 lines arranged in the free Italian form known in Spanish as *silva*. The adjective *primero* has been taken to suggest that Sor Juana, emulating Góngora's two-part *Las soledades* (1613), was planning to write a sequel; however, no record of a companion poem has ever been found.

Margaret Sayers Peden once suggested a different semantic approach. Sor Juana isn't really numbering her poem; instead, she is assuming full responsibility for the act of dreaming: "First I Dream" implies that the anonymous protagonist of the poem, the Soul, is not an abstract entity but a facet of her own self. Sor Juana's piece is about an actual dream and a symbolic one, an intellectual and a poetic quest. Moreover, her quest is multifaceted: a dream about dreaming; a dream about the limits of knowledge; a dream about the possibilities of poetry; and a dream about the antagonism between faith and reason, between received and acquired knowledge, between science and doctrine.

Much has been written about "The Dream" since Ermilo Abreu Gómez's first modern edition of 1928. It is crucial to note that Sor Juana is not actually inventing a new poetic tradition. In fact, epistemological literature in which a dream serves as an excuse to visit the concrete and abstract confines of the universe was common in antiquity. Sor Juana's points of departure and arrival, studied in detail by Paz, Harss, Sabat de Rivers, and José Pascual Buxó, were Cicero's *The Dream of Scipio*, book six of *De re publica*; Kepler's *Somnium, sive Astronomia lunaris*; and, most notably, Athanasius Kircher's *Iter exstaticum coeleste*. After studying Cicero, the early-fifth-century Neoplatonist Ambrosius Macrobius established five categories for dreams: enigmatic, prophetic or visionary, oracular, insomniac, and phantasmal.

Most literary quests were based on the prophetic and the oracular and followed a pattern not unlike that of Dante's *Divine Comedy*, metamorphosed in modern times into what became the bildungsroman: a lost soul first finds a Virgil; together they descend to the underworld; subsequently, they ascend to heaven, where they find enlightenment and peace. Sor Juana's is also a dream of anabasis, or "going up," but is distinct in that the human soul embarks on a solitary journey. The Soul, an androgynous entity represented by a "mournful shadow," separates itself from the bodily prison and travels around and across the earth. First it wanders in the mineral realm; then through the natural; and finally it reaches the celestial spheres, its journey following a Neoplatonist structure, a pyramidal pattern in creation that goes from the simplest item to the most complex.

Since the original text is lost, the issue of how to divide the poem has preoccupied many scholars. Some divide it into twelve major progressive sections, made to resemble the twelve nocturnal hours; others suggest three: sleep, voyage, and awakening. Any way we look at it, faith in a universal order drives the quest, but the end brings only darkness, a clear sign of Sor Juana's increasing skepticism.

The poem has a strong Scholastic, Gnostic, and mystical foundation, but it doesn't parade its erudition in a presumptuous manner. Sor Juana was obviously quite familiar with a vast array of sources. From the Scholastic tradition she drew on Thomism, which sought to reconcile Aristotelian philosophy and Christianity and recognized that the order of universal things could be inferred by studying earthly matters; the teachings of Ramon Llull, who portrayed science as an extension of theology, believed science to be as essential as intuition, and considered empirical and scientific knowledge to be complements of each other; and other Jewish, Muslim, and Christian systems of thought, including those of Averroes, Maimonides, Duns Scotus, and Peter Abelard.

In the Gnostic tradition, Sor Juana was well acquainted with Plotinus, who articulated a vastly influential philosophy based on the linkage and harmonious structure of earthly and celestial realms and whose concepts of "transcendence" and "immanence," approaching creation as a descendant order of things, are pervasive in "The

Dream." And in the mystical tradition she made use of the Kabbalah and Sufism, as well as types of Hermetic Christian systems, positing the link between the divine and human realms by way of arcane connections. Add to these astronomy and the indigenous beliefs Sor Juana derived from the Aztecs and other native Mexican peoples, and the end product is quite an aggregation.

But Sor Juana refuses to endorse any single approach. Instead, in a twist suitable to her Baroque Latin American spirit, she adds and multiplies them, and the resulting syncretism is her signature. Acknowledging this syncretism is crucial to our understanding the poem's overall place in world literature. Its originality is not to be found in the renewal of the literary tradition of dream voyages. Rather, what Sor Juana offers in "The Dream," with a Baroque style more conceptual than that of the rest of her poetry, is a silent challenge to the traditional concept of the Catholic Church. She follows her reason and trusts her faith, but the end result is disappointment: as in the myth of Phaethon, the more we strive to know, the less we understand.

So the question emerges: Was Sor Juana a heretic? The answer is yes and no. Yes, because she dared to question faith at a time and place where Catholic dogma remained intact; no, because she failed to articulate a reformist world view, a critical argument capable of exposing the sham. Bur it was never her goal to do so. As a masterpiece of art, "The Dream" could be written only far from the centers of European knowledge; it is a peripheral work of art generated by the declining echoes of Renaissance thought. Its syncretism is the colonial mask under which it hides. No original philosophical system is offered, only a quilt made of bits and pieces, a sum of disparate parts.

At the same time, Sor Juana comes close to suggesting a type of vision the Enlightenment would deliver in the eighteenth century and beyond: human reason is partial, limited, relative, and unscrupulous; faith, on the other hand, is a palliative to existential doubt, but it offers no real explanation of the ways and mysteries of the cosmos. All this makes the poem unlike anything Santa Teresa de Jesús could deliver, an accumulative pre-Modernist artifact. What's more, for Sor Juana only one aspect of human endeavor emerges triumphant in its quest—poetry.

No concrete reference to it appears, but its power palpitates in each of the poem's words: both *credo* and *episteme*, belief and knowledge, are destined to fail, and divine light cannot cure a broken soul, but the act of writing can bring happiness. Poetry is survival, poetry is the only true redemption, poetry is the door to individualism and self-affirmation. In many ways, "The Dream" is a companion to Sor Juana's *Response to Sor Filotea*, a manifesto promoting freedom of expression and elevating literature to a status higher than all other human affairs, a modernist document transforming poetry into a new type of religion. This subversive spirit explains why Sor Juana is a favorite today: she challenged the ecclesiastical status quo, but with a subtlety that confused her contemporaries; she fought for women's rights, not with weapons, but with poetry.

10

CALAVERA

The period between 1691 and 1693 in Mexico City was marked by heavy rains, floods, famine, and plague. The population blamed the viceroy for their suffering, and Indians stormed the viceregal palace, setting fire to it and to nearby buildings.

In an important biographical essay of 1926, Dorothy Schons writes that on June 8, 1692, "The Viceroy and his wife took refuge in the monastery of St. Francis. Everybody sought monasteries and other places of security. The soldiers were helpless. Hordes of Indians pillaged the plaza and the surrounding neighborhood. Nothing could be done to stop the terrible riot. Bells rang all night. In the nunneries and monasteries prayer was said. Jesuits and Franciscans went in procession to the plaza in an effort to quiet the rioters, but they were hissed and their images were treated with disrespect.

"After days and nights of terror, during which the churches ceased to function, the civil government succeeded in restoring order. Weeks and months of *azotados* [whippings] and *ahorcados* [hangings] kept alive the memory of the tumult." While in retrospect this explosion of violence can be related to the social injustice and racial repression that reigned in New Spain at the end of the seventeenth century, the consensus at the time related the events of "the apocalypse" to "our collective sins." Schons suggests that Sor Juana partially blamed herself for the sad state of affairs: she turned her energy to prayer and to helping convalescent nuns in Santa Paula.

The end of Sor Juana's life brought some surprises. Having given up everything, she apparently had nothing to lose. Some time in 1694 she signed a couple of documents of abjuration—one in blood—and thereby officially renounced humane letters, declared her loyalty to the Catholic faith, repented her sinful actions, and asked the Holy Spirit for forgiveness. "I beg your Sacramental Majesty to grant me license, to all Saints and Angels I ask for mercy, especially those assigned for voting, so that I can be proposed and received by the vote of the entire Celestial Community." Was it another theatrical ploy? Was she truly ashamed? Did she simply accept her fate?

But the inventory at the Convent of Santa Paula evidences a puzzling fact: at the time of her death, Sor Juana, despite her public protestations, still owned about 100 books and some 185 bundles of manuscripts and letters, signaling her ongoing defiance of the Catholic hierarchy. Obviously her spirit had not fully taken *el camino de la perfección*, the road to Christ, as is also indicated by another fact: as the convent's accountant, apparently she had secretly and illegally invested her own funds and those of the institution with a banker.

Rebellion, Albert Camus loved to say, is as easy as saying no. Father Calleja describes Sor Juana's end, when she was risking her health caring for sick nuns during the plague: "The illness was extremely contagious and Sister Juana, by nature compassionate and charitable, attended all [her fellow nuns] without rest and without fear of their proximity. . . . Finally, she fell ill . . . but the severity of the sickness, as extreme as to claim her life, had not the least effect on her mind."

She died during the plague, on April 17, 1695, at the age of forty-six. Her body was buried in the convent's graveyard, supposedly accompanied by the medallion. Her friend and admirer Sigüenza y Góngora delivered the eulogy. According to Paz, Sor Juana's works were salvaged by the Condesa de Paredes.

As she remarked in *A Spiritual Self-Defense*, she had zestfully antagonized the status quo: "Like men, do women not have a rational soul? Why then shall they not enjoy the privilege of the enlightenment of letters? Is a woman's soul not as receptive to God's grace and glory as a man's? Then why is she not able to receive learning and knowledge, which are the lesser gifts?

"What divine revelation, what regulation of the Church, what rule of reason framed for us such a severe law?" And she concluded, "I have this nature; if it is evil, I am the product of it; I was born with it and with it I shall die."

The significance of Sor Juana's journey is best captured by what may be the most memorable sentence she wrote in the *Response to Sor Filotea*: "I suffer no blame, as I have no obligation; no discredit, as I have no possibility of triumphing and *ad impossibilia neme tenetur*." No one is obliged to do the impossible.

The possible, on the other hand, is easier to achieve. In her case, it is achieved through the persistence of pop. Her ubiquity has turned her into an emblem. People seldom know her story. But they know she has power. That is, she has been depersonalized in order to be sanctified. In the interregnum between eternity and the present, her *calavera* is with us forever.

¡Viva la monja!

ACKNOWLEDGMENTS

Gracias to *mi cuate* Frederick Aldama for the suggestion to write this meditation. And to Kristen Buckles at University of Arizona Press for making a home for it. My assistant Sarah Carter deftly handled the process of requesting permissions for the use of the assortment of images. Production was supervised by Amanda Krause. The manuscript was copyedited by Diana Rico. Portions of the material appeared, in somewhat different form, as the introduction to Sor Juana Inés de la Cruz's *Poems, Protest, and a Dream* (Penguin Classics, 1997), translated by Margaret Sayers Peden.

ILLUSTRATION CREDITS

ILAN STAVANS is Lewis-Sebring Professor of Humanities and Latin American and Latino Culture at Amherst College and publisher of Restless Books.